Cloud Dreams

Victoria Lague

Cloud Dreams

Copyright © 2021 Victoria Lague

All rights reserved.

No part of this book may be reproduced or distributed in any manner or form without the written permission from the copyright holder, except in the case of quotations in reviews or articles. The scanning, uploading, and distribution of this book via the Internet or any other means without the permission of the copyright holder is illegal and punishable by law.

ISBN: 13: 9798750784509

First Edition
Keys-Bayfront Publishing, Florida, USA

Dedication

For my readers and friends who encouraged me to write a book of poetry. Be careful what you ask for!

Cloud Dreams

Cloud Dreams

Contents

Acknowledgments	i
Part 1: Within	2
Part 2: Elizabeth Poetry Series	22
Part 3: Without	30

Cloud Dreams

Acknowledgments

Some of the poems in this book were first published online for friends. Many others were written half a lifetime ago for my first creative writing professor. I recently came across the folders of poems, short stories, and essays I wrote in that class, surprisingly preserved after over 45 years, and have included the best ones after some serious revision based on more life experience and the professor's original comments.

I want to thank my online friends for their many encouraging comments that led me to continue writing and posting at least some of my poems online, especially Laurie who was the first to suggest a book of poetry.

The poems in "Part 1: Within" express the poems' speaker in an pensive mood, looking within. The poems in "Part 3: Without" are not meant to be personal; instead, the speaker is functioning universally.

Many of the poems in "Part 2: Elizabeth's Poetry Series" were also first published online for friends and later appeared in my *Unspoken Series* of novels where some of them introduce issues related to particular chapters in *Unspoken 2: After Life*. I wrote the poems for my heroine Elizabeth who is very introspective about her experiences, especially in the first novel in the series that ends with her expressing her intention to write. So, in a way, I have to thank her and the isolation of the Covid-19 Pandemic that left me with a lot of alone time to imagine and write during 2020-2021.

Victoria Lague

Part 1: Within

The Right Place

How was that the right place?
That sad place and dark
Where nothing fit, especially me.
The cold room, metal bed with blankets high
Where I burrowed head first
And folded myself fetal
To cradle my heart, arms crossed,
To protect my gut, knees raised,
Waiting for my body to build heat in my tent
Breathing in warmth my sobs to vent.
Whose error dropped me there,
That sad place and dark?
The wrong place it must have been,
And the right place lost to me.
Was that the right place,
That sad dark alone place?
Was that the place for me to be
Without support or direction?
In my lonely state marking time
Nothing to show I'm loved or wanted?
Someone, but not me, worth time and affection.
What was wrong with me?
Existing in that crumbling place, but wanting to be me,
Withdrawing inside to protect myself, pining to be free.
Unnerved by the world, retreating within
Yet watching without for hints of how to be

Acceptable, presentable
In a world where I cannot see home.

And then one day the right place,
A concrete gray and stark place
To belong, be home, smile and be free.
People who saw me, liked me too,
My value recognized, my contributions true.
No huddled warmth my sobs to vent,
But joyful and bright with smiles of our content.
Someone who liked me more than a little bit.
An attraction complete with affection and friendship.
No longer lost, but finally home.

~~~

Seasons

Spring & Summer

I found you when I was green
And your Autumn colors dazzled me
Through my Spring and my Summer too
Your Autumn hid Winter from you
Our ages gapped but
Your Autumn filled me and
My Summer fed you
We joined in joyful desire
Together we satisfied needs unmet
Apart we struggled until Winter found you
And abandoned me to Autumn
Desolate

Autumn & Winter

Hindsight lacks mercy
I was going to him sometime soon
But others intervened
With a snag patched and fixed
Now I weather the gloom of unknowing
And we have to wait anew

Going would have been easy
Waiting is hard
Not knowing when or how
Getting through the wreck of life
The rest and the test of life
Through the dreaded Autumn
Toward the desolate Winter
Alone
Those slips along the ice
The inevitable thrum of the fixed drum
That keeps me from going to you

Waiting is hard
Wondering if the fix will hold
And other horrors await
Or if the fix will fold
Unexpectedly taking me late
Waiting is hard
Dying will be simple

~~~

Mother's Day

To all the mothers who revel today
You with your children
And grands sweet and gay

Victoria Lague

Enjoy every moment
Gather them in your arms
Against the day they are absent
Hold them to your hearts
Memorize each curve, each smile
Against the day you must depart
But, for today
Happy Mother's Day

To all who do not rejoice today
Your choice without children
Or grands sweet and gay
Hold your decision in your hearts
Your choice, right to make
Live the life you love
Look ahead though the future be opaque
And, for today
Happy (Un)mother's Day

To all we would-be mothers today
Short-changed by vulgar nature
No grands sweet and gay
No children for comfort in our age
Perhaps, alone without our loves
Watching the tributes that don't assuage
Act not against the joys we've had
Hold them to our hearts
Memorize each curve, and smile
For our joys shall not depart
And, for today
Live

~~~

The Questions of Fathers

Whom do I celebrate today?
The man who made me,
Frustrated with the me I was, or
The man who made me,
Pleased with the me I could be?

Whom do I celebrate today?
The man who denied my need to be me, or
The man who filled a need he could see?

Whom do I celebrate today?
The man who created an empty space, or
The man who often filled it with grace?

Could the second have flourished without the first?

Whom do I celebrate today?
Should I reject the second benign and
Favor the first as mine?
I reject the first's discouraging nay, yet
Accept my life as coming from him.
I treasure the second's encouraging faith and
Assert my heart as thoroughly his.
He is the one I honor today:
The man who helped me find my way.

~~~

Awakening

How to dispel the gloom of all these weeks:
A forest closed from the sky,
No sun peeking through whispering leaves,
No stars lighting my way in the dark

Until my spirit guide arrives
Invisible beside me,
And then I step back to make way.
I invite him to take my space within,
His energy gently encircling.

What is the most important thing
I need to know right now?

I wait in anticipation for words only he can provide.
He answers with susurrant breaths
That dispel the darkness inside.
My guide speaks with authority:
Trust.
Do not doubt.
Know.
Trust him, your beloved,
My guide does strongly advise.

I respond to the words I had once known,
The words swallowed in the dark,
By the gloom beneath the leaves,
By the pulp beneath the bark,
And I respond to him,
My guide, who exudes peace and calm.

I do trust my beloved.
Their words cannot hurt me,
Or make me into something I'm not,
Or replace his memory with ruinous rot.
My guide's peace and calm are mine.

I sleep in memory tonight.
I dream unknown dreams and
Awaken to their shadows

Lingering in my eye.
My beloved is here, joyful in me,
Gentle and sweet in his love.
The sun breaks through the star-studded sky.
The words press the ebbing gloom
And live again, bright in my joyous mind.

~~~

The Old Photo

The old photo found
Fading into gentle sepia
Me in a white sweater
Pulled over ample curves
V-neck edged with ruffle
And tresses of cascading curls.
Today I see it
What he saw that night
Studying my face
While I wondered, what?
Candlelight steadily flowing
Dropping a dimming twilight
Into a pedestrian room
Turned into sweet bower
Where he first sees me
Yet not the first
Not in this way at least.
He moved across the room
Determined and engrossed
Amazement and questions
Living on his face.
Observation intense
Eyes targeted
Unflinching
Drawn to the center

In the ring of my irises
His searching eyes to mine.
His gentle gaze caressed my face
Swept across my dark hair
The arch of my brows
Down the curve of my nose
To the fullness of my lips
Amid the swell
Of cheeks and chin.
I followed his darting eyes
His ocular caresses and
Silent search intent on studying me.

But what he found in my face
Remained a mystery
Like plumbing the depths
Of the vast ocean floor
The far stretches of constellations
Or the enigma of the soul.
Until the old photo found
Revealed his mystery to me.
The coy tip of my head
And sideways glance of my eyes
The smile suggesting innocence
But promising more.
Qualities I had not perceived
Living on my face.
This is what his searching found
His study fruitful and rewarding
Touching his heart
Fresh and profound
My ocean of love
My glowing star of youth
The enigma of my soul
Exposed for him to see.

Overwhelmed

You overwhelmed me
Eyes
Looking down in shades of blue
Brightest ocean waves
Hair near black
Extracting my sigh
Stooping to my height
Gazing deeply eye to eye

You overwhelmed me
Hands
Clasped before you in prayer
Asking only a simple thing
Close to your heart's song
That more and more my heart did sing

Cradling my hands
A soft gentle fleeting time
Your blest kiss lingers forever
A sweet puzzle you made sublime

Strong hands reaching
Love veiled my astonished face
Drawn into outstretched arms
Giving freely in joyous grace

You overwhelmed me
Body
Slender muscles well defined
Always gentle with tender restraint
A caress so pleasant it stole my breath and
My conscious mind was moved to faint

You Have No Idea

You don't know the best thing that happened to me

He supported and encouraged my education
He validated me
I was a person worth knowing
He became the parental influence I needed
Chatting about nothing particular
Spending time together
Getting to know each other
He became the friendly influence I needed
The strong courageous military man
The brilliant witty paternal man
The tall dark and handsome man
I admired him

He noticed little things
My fingernail scratching my neck into red irritation
My poorly hidden arousal during classroom discussion
My unexpected daydream that attracted his attention
He validated me
I was a woman worth knowing
No belittling my aspirations
No offensive denigrations or alleged imperfections
Carrying my books between classrooms instead
No one had shown me such affection
I adored him

He kissed my hand
Gazed into my eyes
Invited me for coffee
No glimpse of rejection or words to eschew

Cloud Dreams

He chose me
For the first time I trusted and he was true
I loved him
He was so sweet and handsome
Wrapped in his white lab coat over a dark suit
Adorned with a plaid bow tie matching his eyes so blue
Attracting my eye walking by my class all new
Smiling together through a wall of glass
The time he checked on me teaching class

He was so sweet and handsome
Bedecked in black tails and
Bronze not explained
Adorned with white bow tie and
Black hair turned grey
Only a moment to spend after primping so fine
Thinking of me then driving to see
Kissing hello and smiling goodbye
After showing himself off to me

You don't know the slice of life
The happy slice we carved as one
The line we walked between us and blood

Delighted when he arrived
Smiling and happy to share a kiss
Laughing upstairs and smiling down
He chose me alone
Voicing words he was mine to revere
The last week mine though he was not near
That day mine because he was there
My sweet love swathed in my total caress
Happiness transformed into glorious bliss
The only joy I've ever known
I chose him and he chose me alone

Victoria Lague

~~~

Standing by Your Grave

The first time was horrific
Not to be believed
How could you be dead?
Even weeks after later
I looked down in disbelief
I wanted
To cover your grave with my body
To protect you from rain and cold
To hide the gravestone that must be lying
To end, there and then, with you
Instead of standing by your grave

The second time I approached with excitement
Yet, something stabbed at me
With mystical points from
From a hundred bayonets
As I was standing by your grave

The third time was peaceful
A time for me to talk sweetly to you
I promised
To return sooner than twenty years
To remember everyone you loved
To allow you to haunt my dreams
To wait for you there when I cannot
Be standing by your grave

The fourth time approached
For me to visit you
Who was brilliant and witty
With a distinct turn of phrase
That only you could voice

Cloud Dreams

Who was sweet and gentle
With a smile and kiss
That only you could give
Who was courageous and brave
The strongest man I've ever known
I stooped to brush leaves from your stone
And ran my fingers along your name and honors
I buried a small fossil brought from home
Just beneath the grass near your stone
So part of my life is always with you
As your crest is always with me when I
Am not standing by your grave

The fifth time like the third again
I walked to the wall and
Finding your name among the rest
Memorialized in polished stone
I ran my fingers softly on
Graven letters that betoken you
And all things achieved and affected
Your service, family, and me
Like the engraving in granite
On this heroes' wall
Your name is always with me
Engraved on my heart and
Alive in my thoughts when I
Am not standing by your grave

The sixth time began the night before,
Quietly positioning a Samhain meal
Two settings for me and you.
Only my chair occupied that I could see,
But in spirit you sat across from me.
No physical presence that I could define,
But your spirit was with me as we dined.
I moved to the sofa and closed my eyes.

I breathed in, exhaled, my thoughts to revise.
Your spirit remained with me.
I felt your peace as a silken mantle
Descending and thoroughly gentle.
I carried your peace the following day
When roses on your grave I laid
And checked the buried fossil above your name,
And turned in pensive silence
Then turned around again
To touch your stone, my love,
As I was standing by your grave.

The seventh time fresh roses I laid
I turned around and made to walk
'Til his waving arm said he wanted to talk.
"Thank you for your service," he said.
My service is nil I thought.
"Is your husband buried in this place," he asked.
"Yes," I replied, my thoughts unmasked.
The nameless man, the disheveled man,
His words were part of your Samhain plan.
"Be sure to speak to him everyday."
"I do," I assured him, "*every* day."
I speak to you morning and night, I knew.
I speak to you waking and sleeping, too.
Be sure to say you love him wholly
The old man's story urged.
Be sure to tell him you love him truly.
And with "God bless you," he ended his words.
I returned his blessing and walked away
Wondering aloud how he came to be,
Arriving and speaking his testament,
Acknowledging your spirit with me
As I was standing by your grave.

And after the last time

Whenever that may be
I'll wait for you, Beloved
I'll wait for you to come for me.

~~~

Why?

Should one woman denigrate another's love?
Because she is somehow effected?
Because she labels my pleasure immoral?
Because she finds a natural bodily fusion
Unacceptable to her?
Not to be desired?
Why?
Does he have to be labeled a predator?
Is it wrong for him to
Want me, choose me, claim me
The only way he could?
Should I have tried to
Fight him off
Beg him to stop
When I wanted everything too?
Not knowing how to tell him my need.
He initiated and I, so fearful, followed his lead.
Why?

I think back now
Amused by the tension that filled me.
Something I wanted, yet feared.
Struck dumb by my own innocence with
No knowledge how to please,
No experience how to ask,
No trust in anyone but him.

Why did I know nothing?

Where does that blame lie?
Myself for my own innocence?
A mother who spoke sans significance
Denigrating my body, not guiding my youth?
Expecting me to be a forever child
Without pleasure however mild?
Society and culture that denigrate female desire?
A woman's pleasure as immoral?
Sensuality as disgusting?
To be denied?
Eliminated?
Surely I was only showing my humanity.

The issue was not forced.
Desire was attached to caring.
The long wait before the act.
The man I wanted though
I knew little of what wanting meant.
The man I loved who guided me through
My shyness and fear.
Letting him who had only kissed my hand touch me.
We yearned for that connection.
He demanded and insisted
In the powerful strength of his embrace,
Restrained and restricted.
The stunning surprise.
The moments to decide.
I would give up nothing,
Do it all again.
Enjoy the beauty and wonder of it,
My head resting against his chest.
His arm tight around me.
A gentle nudge of guidance.
Joyful experience in the forceful pursuit.
Strong embrace,
Heated kiss,

Probing hands,
Affectionate smile,
All that we relished in gratitude
In the long awaited evening light.
When part of him became part of me.

~~~

Miami

Where would I be if not here?
Having sweated out my life
In the blasting textile heat, or
On my first floor confined
The second unattainable with
Endangered aging knees, or
Living in my parents' old house
Disintegrating beneath my feet
Three possible toxic lives
Without the one I needed to meet

Instead I'm under a dazzling star
Ocean breezes from afar
Azure skies the days adorn
Pearly clouds the horizon crowns
Memory sustains
Beyond the loss of him
Thought abides
Declaring love still true
Hope remains
His face one day to see
Calm resides
Flowing from him to me

~~~

Victoria Lague

Regret

Frailty looked me in the face one day
Speaking of pasts lost and futures not yet arisen

My grandmother's white face and labored breathing
Words of her tortured past had bubbled out
All the pains of yesterdays that never healed
Held tight inside her head and heart
Like the prized moments of her life
The demons of her lengthy life
Possessing her final days

A lesson learned?
Must I learn to let my memories end
So no possessing demons rule my old age
Let the tortures take their toll and move on
Leaving me with time to heal?

Seeing my grandmother's burdened past
I saw myself ladened with age
My age filled with the past, like hers

Should I make the choice she once refused
Let each experience slowly express
My present gliding from then to now
From now to tomorrow with
Nothing to lament?

Or, should I hold to my heart
Each moment of love and passion
No matter how burdensome they may weigh
No matter the loss of moments
That mattered more than I can say?
Like her, I choose to hold them close
Without regret

Turning into Grandma

The face in the mirror is no longer mine
With unexpected stealth
My mother's slid into its place
Unnoticed
Masking the girl-face that was mine while
The weight of the years
The gravity of time
Etched themselves beside the smile in my eyes
And the upturned corners of my mouth,
Pointing the way south for everything that followed
Covertly, my mother's face replaced mine
But I never noticed
Then one day when the face in the mirror looked back
I saw the creeping image of my mother had edged in
I looked more like her than myself
With my grey hair and sagging eyelids.
My great-grandmother once told her granddaughter
"The first things that goes are your hands"
One day, those words had new meaning for me
They flooded into my nightmare consciousness that
Continues every day when I inspect what's left of me.
I look at my hands and see spots that are not freckles and
Extra wrinkles etched by years of grasping knuckles
When did those ridges in my pinky nail start forming
I never noticed

This was the conversation my mother and I never had
Though my mother once told me,
"I've turned into my mother" and

For an instant the face before me in the mirror
Was Grandma not Mom then back
Mom with thin mousy hair instead of vibrant red
With hooded eyelids partly hiding the startling green
With the dowager's hump that laid
The heaviness of age upon her
And when did I become so much taller than she
I never noticed

So, time continues its dirty work
And I remind myself to stand tall
Even when my back wants to curl itself into a knot
And my neck wants release from the weight of my head
I swab my face with cream each night
And tinted cream each morning
Yes, I look more like myself
I try to recapture the rich brown and
Too-thick hair of my youth
But to my consternation I can replace it
Only with Clairol and a short cut
Meanwhile, my grandmother's image waits
Somewhere on the other side of my mirror
To silently slide in place over mine
Even the echoes of my mother's face
Will be hidden by the mask of hers
Slowly
Over time
When will the scheming remodel commence
I will never even notice

~~~

My Laughing Space

When I was young in another place
I climbed up the wooded hill and

Cloud Dreams

Tried to balance on rusted rails
Where the train traveled true
But I always fell

I slid down sanded slopes
Where beneath the piney wood
I tried to swim the river
But I never could

I tried to make friends with everyone
To be what they were, succumb to their laws and tried
To be a part of their lives
But I never was

So when I was young in that other place
With problems such as these
I ran off through the countryside
To a quiet place
My laughing space
Where I only had to be me

I walked across the springy ground
Layered needles of scented pine
I listened to the hidden brook
And the chirping birds sublime
I settled down beneath a pine
The largest I could find
And leaned my head against the tree
Relaxed and safe in
My quiet place
My laughing space
Where I was free to be only me

~~~

Victoria Lague

Virgin Galactic

I drop my coins on
The online counter
Of Omaze
And watch the receipt
Appear in the digital handler
Of my email
My coins released
To realize the oldest
Of my dreams
To experience the
Rising pressure in the coldest
Of gravity extremes
That will press the chest
Along with the spine
Of my being
Inside the suit
To the cradling shrine
Of my hoping
The silent purchase
Mimics the noise
Of my dream
I want to hear the
Indifferent black poise
Of space seem
An impregnable
Amazing counterpoise
In the extreme
As I'm learning how
To walk again to move
Completely
Pressing my hands and
Face to the window
Concretely
Touching the face of space

Cloud Dreams

And the staring eyes that
Twinkle no more
I want to feel the
Sudden descent as
I am drawn to the floor
Of my existence
I want to see the
Final approach to the door
Of my resistance
When I return to my
Mundane life and the roar
Of life's persistence
Yes the ticket will be worth
The coins that I pour
For online assistance
If I can see amazing Earth
That I can adore
From that distance

Part 2: Elizabeth's Poetry Series

1-Consent

The cosmos has a wry sense of humor
Birthing us a generation apart
Our separate destinies it did maneuver
For us, no passing in the dark

You survived the army, an officer
Returned safe and apt
You chose to teach thereafter
I chose to learn then, by you enrapt

Surely Professor and oftentimes Da
Support and affirmation flow
Paternal heart in a surrogate father
Healer of wounds inflicted long ago

Always Friend and lastly Lover
The spark for our heat and mutual fire
From quiet attraction a nascent ardor
Ignited a smoldering flame of desire

You waited long for the ready time
When you were eager and I was ripe
Once so effortless to decline
But now conceding the time was right

Boldly assuaging your hunger
Control and direction your design
Restraint and embrace full measure
Serenity and consent were mine

~~~

2-Light

I grew accustomed to your light
The smile lines across your face and
Fringed corners of your eyes
The azure blue that lit them and
The sparkle that made them bright
The special stare that focused
My attention day or night
Its trance-inducing aspect
I lost myself inside
The silent glow and flow of courage
The vigor of our desire
Whatever you might ask of me
Amenable was I

~~~

3-Grief

Grief still sneaks up
Unexpectedly
Awaiting my most fragile moment
When I think I am well
When my heart is overflowing with you
Filled with warmth and soft feelings
That grief can hold on to
And tear into
With sharp razor fangs

Victoria Lague

To slice flesh and heart
Blood spilling from eyes
That see only you
My desire and blessing
Lifting my soul
Yearning only for you
My love and comfort
Encircle me
Who has loved no man but you

~~~

4-Sweet Music

My heart yearns to dance to sweet music

To feel
the rush of tropical winds
the rumble of tectonic plates
the Earth's swirling molten core

To touch
the progress of pulsing stars
the roar of nebulas
the songs of celestial spheres

To hear
our hearts' blood surging
our warm breaths mingling
your dear voice breathing my name

To devour each the other
the heat of bodies
the sigh of breaths
the fibers of bone and skin

To taste
the blessed passion
the delectable flash and
the joyful coda

To coalesce and ripen into
melodious music
hallowed harmony
A dance emerging from our bodies

To compose
The sweet music of our souls

~~~

5-Alongside Grief, Panic

Panic threatens a deluge
Seeking
Persisting
Inundating
Engulfing
Submerging-
A tidal wave after an earthquake
A storm surge over the land
A bridge collapsing in raging waters
A flood of waves over ancient trees
Salty inundation complete
Then
Receding
Subsiding
Evaporating
Exposing-
A salty rind emerges
A white-encrusted wound

Hard and pitted
Raised rim catching and tearing
Reveals the trauma beneath
Until the flood returns
Dissolving the rind
And beginning the cycle anew

~~~

6-His Memory

I live in the sun of his memory

Once
He drew from my essence and
I feasted on his
We moved as one entwined
We sighed as one
Yet not coeval
Paternal blessings in his smile
He affirmed affection with his eyes
And won adoration in mine
We breathed the same air
We craved one flesh
Too soon hindered by time

I sleep in the arms of his memory

Tonight
He brings his astral essence
The energy of cosmos refined
Our senses enhance
We sigh as one
Though still not coeval
Loving blessings in my hand
He affirms affection in his eyes

And adoration in his stance
We breath the same air
We join to combine
A new coupling of spirit and flesh

~~~

7-A Comfort to Me

How could I have known
When I wept at the loss
That his memory would emerge
Like new leaves sprouting
In the spring of long Covid days

With memories sweet
A loving warmth spreads
His vaporous arm encircles
A gentle hand cups my cheek
Turning my head to settle
On a shoulder strong and tender
Allowing my breath to speak
My tension to abate
In the safety of his embrace
Moving me to slumber sweet
Where we talk àmidst the fray
And I survive another solitary day

~~~

8-Acceptance

What is it like to be the last one standing?
The one who can look back
And see the way of it all?

The tall, handsome man,
The one who first saw me,
The man I dared to notice, and
Once seen, could not deny,
The man who became
My first and my last
In a closet of a different kind.

The beautiful woman
Whose lover I shared,
Known only to him and me,
Or perhaps,
Whose freedom from him
Blossomed because of me.

And when I'm no longer standing,
Having moved to that other plane,
Perfected with understanding,
Will she accept our great
Shared love and smile?
Then, let him walk between us,
Claim us with fingers entwined,
Three together, accepting,
In love and thoughts aligned.

~~~

9-Cloud Dream

In the safety of my cloud dream
I curl in a waking sleep
The vaporous cloud surrounds me
Supports me from beneath

It billows upward growing
Soft white with a tinge of blue

Cloud Dreams

Above me the sky is fading
And suddenly the cloud is you.

Your arms are wrapped around me
I feel your peace and heat
Your serenity overwhelms me
Your love and my love meet

In the cradle of your arms I sigh
Feeling your calm unique
Radiating love engulfs my soul
As I savor this beautiful dream

Part 3: Without

For Marjorie, 1984

I suppose I was just feeling my mortality too,
But there was nothing "just" that Friday,
The day Marjorie died.

In my mind, I can see and hear
The last smile and words
That came my way
Before the day Marjorie died.

How sad a life that's stolen
Leaving an empty depression
In place of tomorrow's promise
Like the day that Marjorie died

Painful enough to die
But how grievous the pain
From a futile death by fire
The appalling plunge to earth
Like the day that Marjorie died

Death sets the trap
Each of us will trip the wire
Lose the mastery of our own lives
Become Death's fresh prey
Like the day that Marjorie died

It is decreed
Circumvention is not allowed
Plan what you will but know
Your plans are unavailing
Death stalks
Like the day that Marjorie died

~~~

Inertia

Motivation must come from without
When the motivating factor within is wanting
And our bootstraps lay in some remote region
Where inertia reigns
Easy to remain inert where
One week glides into the next
Matures into a month of fatuous days
And a new disorder becomes unplanned routine
But each innocent novelty can
Raze the entire system
A malevolent mutation
A tormenting thorn
A lethal gash
A bull in the China shop
Destroying the inaction within us
Bullheaded bulwark of the status quo
Inertia is
Pretending change retired
And moved south for the winter
There has been no retirement
Change moves around the inertia-bound
And finally from within
Desire breaks free to join the party
Dethroning inertia
To make us free

Victoria Lague

~~~

Coming of Age

He preached his politics and
Challenged our people to dream
Opened their hearts
Opened their minds

That year ~ the infamous year ~
We came of age and
Once we dared to dream again
We soared and fell to earth
And splattered our dreams in suburbia

But, now others collect the pieces
Fit them together in jigsaw fashion
And challenge us to reconstruct

Where was compassion entombed
Where did peace find its fragmented resting place
Each of these needs only the right words
To flower again and
Challenge our people to dream

~~~

Becoming

I went walking today on sponge-wet path
Round the alfalfa growing in spurts
Set between clods of earth

Soon the green will o'ertake the brown
The brilliant yellow of dandelions

Cloud Dreams

Will age to a hoary fluff
Fly to other lands with
Only the bitter leaves left behind

They will melt into the rest
A carpet of new pink wildflowers
And speckled green
A garden of bees
The spirits of grasses will line the path
Magnificent in emerald glory

The path of freedom
The greatest of parables
One need only look to see
Words written in the colors of what is
Splendor surrounding me there today
As life commences its marvelous rebirth

In my mind I already see the field that will be
Pink and yellow speckling the view
Bees busy living among the green
Ever so slowly moving to their finale
Yet that truth does not deter them
From the hope of new pollen
And sweeter flowers

And everyday I will make my passage
Rereading the parable as it transmutes
Unwittingly becoming part of my surroundings
Inseparable and soul-immersed
A sliver of the parable I read

About The Author

I began my literary career studying creative writing at Rhode Island Junior College, later renamed Community College of Rhode Island where I earned an A.A. degree in Liberal Studies in 1975, earned my A.B. at Brown University in English and American Literature in 1977, and my M.A. in English Literature from Rhode Island College, 1982, specializing in Arthurian Literature. I taught literature and academic writing for over 10 years at Community College of Rhode Island while also working in the banking industry. Eventually, I accepted a position teaching composition and literature at Miami Dade College's Kendall Campus.

I was named Outstanding Teacher in the community colleges category by the South Atlantic Modern Language Association in 1998, was honored for my teaching by the Florida Association of Community Colleges (now the Florida Association of Colleges) in 2001, and was awarded the Rosenberg, McIntosh, Leigh Endowed Teaching Chair at Miami Dade College in 2002. I retired from teaching in 2017.

Now I spend my time writing poems and short fiction, designing and sewing my own clothes, and making quilts.

Also By Victoria Lague

Novels:

Unspoken Series
Unspoken 1: Life Happens
Unspoken 2: After Life
Unspoken 3: More Life

Olivia's Boys

Out of Print Textbooks:
Formulas for Composition, 4 editions
Kendall Hunt Publishing

Made in the USA
Columbia, SC
13 November 2021